How To Sell An Internet Business

A Quick Legal Guide

2nd Edition

by Mike Young, Esq.

Copyright Notice

Table of Contents

How To Use This Guide

Each Quick Legal Guide™ is designed as a resource for you to quickly learn the most important things you need to know about one business legal topic.

In the *Introduction* section, we'll provide an overview of the essential steps to selling your Internet business.

In *Chapter 1*, we'll discuss the key players you'll want to put on your sales team to maximize the price you'll get while protecting yourself from liability.

Then we'll identify how to determine your asking price in *Chapter 2*.

In *Chapter 3*, we'll help you identify the type of sale you want to do, weighing the pros and cons of each method. And we'll show you how to pre-qualify prospective buyers to save yourself time.

Learn how to review a buyer's offer in *Chapter 4*. And how to get compensated for lost time if a deal falls apart before closing.

Chapter 5 reveals what you should expect a prospective buyer to do as part of due diligence prior to closing on the deal. And what you can do to prepare to meet requests for information.

In Chapter 6, we'll cover how closing typically occurs for the sale of an online business. And common closing documents you should expect to see.

Finally, you'll learn about post-closing tasks in Chapter 7 you'll want to make sure get done to prevent legal and financial problems later.

The guide also contains a *Quick Start Checklist* so you know what to do after reading the guide.

Additional material, including a *Resources* section, is located at the back of this guide. These reference materials should be used as-needed but aren't essential to understanding the topic.

Introduction - Your Sales Roadmap

Here's a brief overview of the steps you'll want to take to successfully sell your ecommerce company.

First, you'll build your sales team. In addition to yourself, your team should include: a reputable Internet business broker, an accountant or tax planner who understands ecommerce, and an experienced Internet business lawyer.

Second, you will work with your team to determine a realistic asking price. Realistic means a fair value on the high end based on actual financial numbers rather than emotions or other subjective means that are hard to quantify.

Third, you will decide what type of transaction you're willing to do from a legal standpoint. Will you sell your equity in the existing company? Or will you keep the equity and sell some or all of the company's assets instead?

Fourth, you'll set the criteria for prequalifying prospective purchasers of your ecommerce company. This reduces the chance you'll be wasting your time with unqualified prospects or sharing your confidential information with people who should not have it.

Fifth, you will review offer(s) made to purchase your Internet business, decide whether to accept an offer, or make a counteroffer. In many cases, you'll be reviewing an offer that's contained in a prospective buyer's nonbinding letter of intent (LOI) to purchase.

Sixth, if you accept an offer or a prospect accepts your counteroffer, you will be cooperating with the prospect during a due diligence phase while the prospect reviews information before going forward with closing on the deal.

Seventh, you will close on the deal with the assistance of your sales team. In most cases, you'll never meet the buyer face-to-face because the buyer is located in another city, state, or even a different country.

Finally, you and your team will work with the buyer to do various post-closing activities per your agreement. This can include paperwork related to the transfer of assets or equity, escrow activities, and/or advising the buyer for a period of time after the sale takes place.

Chapter 1 - Your Sales Team

Your Business Broker

An experienced Internet business broker can help you sell your ecommerce company easier and on better terms than you will be able to do by yourself. Among other things, your broker will help you prep the business so you can maximize the sales price. Plus, a good broker will actively market your company to prospective qualified buyers.

If confidentiality is important so that your competitors and customers don't know you're looking to sell, your broker can market your company without revealing it by name. After pre-screening and a nondisclosure agreement (NDA) has been signed by a prospect, the broker will reveal the particular details.

So how do you pay for a business broker?

Most reputable Internet brokers will work on a commission basis. This means they get paid a percentage of the sale price when your ecommerce company is sold.

Beware of a broker who demands to be paid up front for services that may never be rendered. You should also avoid retaining a broker who wants to represent the buyer too in the sale of your Internet business because there's too much of a conflict of interest even if the broker agrees to split his fees between you and the buyer.

Reputable business brokers will ask you to sign a written contract that explains what they will do for you and how they will get paid. Be sure to have your Internet lawyer take a look at any provisions you don't understand or want changed before you sign the agreement.

In the *Resources* section at the back of this guide, you'll find a list of Internet business brokers with their contact information. You may wish to start there in your search for a broker to represent you.

Your Tax Planner & Accountant

Although your Internet business lawyer will assume the primary role of protecting you from legal dangers, your tax planner/accountant should know your financial situation better than your attorney.

This means you'll want to bring your accountant or tax planner into the sales process as soon as possible so he can work with your Internet lawyer to structure the sale in a way that maximizes your profit, minimizes your taxes, and does so in a way that reduces the chance you'll get hit with a tax audit in the process.

Your Internet Business Lawyer

Retaining an experienced Internet ecommerce attorney before you even get a broker involved is important in order to protect your interests, ensure you get what you want from the sale of your online business, and avoid expensive lawsuits and tax audits.

Your Internet lawyer should focus on ecommerce law with experience representing buyers and sellers of privately held Internet companies. This experience will be put to good use to make sure the contracts and other legal documents you sign (e.g. broker's agreement, agreement of sale, escrow agreement, etc.) will include provisions designed to help you achieve your goals from the sale while protecting you in the process.

Chapter 2 - Determining Your Asking Price

Determining the true value of your online company is an art. As a privately held venture, there isn't a public market of traded shares to look at for even guesstimating what your business is worth. What you consider important about your company may be very different than the primary reason a prospective purchaser wants to own your business.

Working with your sales team, you can ascertain an asking price as well as your bottom line that you're willing to accept. However, these numbers may not tell the full story. The true value is what a qualified buyer will pay. All the rest is theoretical.

That being said, there must a factual basis for your asking price because prospective buyers will want to know how you arrived at the number you want them to pay.

Revenues

One quick valuation technique is to calculate monthly or annual revenues and then ask for a multiple of that number.

However, revenues do not equal profitability. There are many Internet businesses, particularly those with venture capital funding or angel investors, that run at a loss while ramping up during their start-up phase, i.e. there has never been a profit.

If your business model is rapid growth with the hope of profitability and a big payout in the future, this may describe your revenues.

Unfortunately, this doesn't make your Internet business attractive except perhaps to a large company that wants to acquire your assets for reasons other than short-term profitability (e.g. intellectual property, key personnel, etc.). These types of acquisitions are relatively rare.

Earnings

Instead of revenues, your prospects will likely be more concerned with earnings because the buyer wants income.

Privately held Internet businesses are often valued by prospective purchasers at 1 to 3 times annual earnings. This may include looking at your Internet business' discretionary earnings by removing certain expenses you currently incur that the buyer can eliminate.

If you're using a *multiple of revenues* to determine your asking price, you should also calculate discretionary earnings too so you have a fall-back position to justify the company's valuation. Calculating by both methods also puts you on firmer ground when negotiating with a prospective buyer.

For example, if a prospect makes a low offer based on a multiple of earnings without taking into account discretionary expenses, you can quickly respond by showing how much more your business is worth by explaining why actual earnings are truly higher when the discretionary expenses are taken into account.

Structuring Your Payments

It's common for a qualified prospective purchaser to make an offer consisting of multiple payments over time instead of a single lump sum payment for the purchase price at closing.

Depending upon your circumstances, it *may* make financial sense to accept a portion of the sales price post-closing as a means to legally reduce your tax liability.

However, you should work with your Internet lawyer to ensure there are incentives in place for the purchaser to actually pay what's owed under the deal. This may include holding certain assets in escrow until payment in full is received by you.

It rarely makes sense to base your payments in part on an earn-out where you're required to stay active in the company post-sale for a year or more.

Unless you're getting paid additional compensation for such services, this type of earn-out essentially means you will be free labor for the purchaser because part of the company's sales price is covering your work. After all, you could be investing your time and expertise elsewhere and getting paid for it.

Chapter 3 - Determine The Type of Sale

When you sell your Internet business, the transaction will be structured as either an equity or an asset sale. Working with your sales team, you should have identified ahead of time which type of transaction makes the most sense for you prior to listing the company for sale.

However, it is common for a prospective buyer to come back with a counteroffer that varies from the original terms on major issues, including the type of sale.

You should understand the pros and cons of each type of transaction because you want to make an informed decision whether to sell equity or assets. For tax purposes, how the transaction is structured may affect capital gains tax liability.

Equity Sale

If you sell the equity in your ecommerce company, the purchaser becomes the new owner of the legal entity that owns the business assets.

For example, if you are the sole shareholder of ABC Tech Corp., an equity sale would involve you transferring your corporate stock to the buyer.

There are some benefits to both parties to an equity transaction (e.g. less paperwork) And because the same entity owns the assets, there should be few issues regarding the buyer emailing company lists without violating spam laws or using licensed intellectual property (software, stock photography, etc.).

However, few prudent buyers will agree to an equity purchase because of potential hidden liabilities within the company. This can include debt collection, contract obligations, and lawsuits arising from transactions that took place before the equity was sold.

Asset Sale

Most sales of Internet businesses are done as asset sales. This means the purchaser's limited liability company (LLC) or corporation will buy some or all of your company's *assets* but not the equity in your company.

As a seller, it may make sense for you to have an asset sale if multiple ecommerce ventures are owned and operated under a single legal entity but only one of the ventures will be sold. For example, let's say your company owns five profitable ecommerce websites in different niches but decides to sell only one of them. The assets for the one website can be sold while your entity retains ownership of the assets for the other four sites.

For the buyer, an asset sale makes it possible to purchase only the resources truly needed to keep the Internet business running. For instance, if your entity has office space, vehicle leases, and computer equipment not needed by the purchaser, your entity may keep those assets and liabilities as part of the deal.

Prequalifying Prospective Purchasers

When an Internet business is offered for sale, there's usually a brief listing (from one paragraph to one page) that describes the company without naming it. The listing may or may not include your asking price.

It's common to receive many inquiries from unqualified prospects, particularly from people who would like to own businesses in the abstract but lack the financial resources to do so.

Regardless of their motives, they *will* waste your time.

You need to filter these unqualified people out of the sales process. A good business broker will help you do this efficiently. This can include using pre-screening questionnaires or even setting buyer net worth requirements (e.g. an accredited investor) in the listing itself that must be met before more detailed information about the company (e.g. a prospectus) will be provided to a potential buyer.

Confidentiality

Prospective qualified buyers should be required to sign a written nondisclosure agreement (NDA) before receiving certain information about your company. The timing for signing the NDA will vary depending upon your needs.

If you're trying to keep customers and competitors from knowing you've placed your ecommerce company up for sale by a blind listing through a business broker, chances are you'll want the NDA signed by a prospect during the prequalification process.

Regardless, a signed NDA should be in place before you release any important company information to a prospective buyer whether or not an offer has been made. Information you will want to protect includes trade secrets, financials, customer information, business plans, and other confidential data.

Your Internet lawyer can provide you with an NDA for qualified prospects to sign before you make disclosures. However, dishonest people will ignore a contract's terms (including an NDA). If you believe a prospect is dishonest, it's better to trust your gut and wait for another prospective buyer than to have an NDA signed but violated.

Chapter 4 - Reviewing an Offer to Buy Your Business

Letter of Intent (LOI)

After a prospective buyer has preliminarily evaluated your business and decided to move forward, the next step is to submit an offer to purchase. The most common way to do this is through a non-binding letter of intent (LOI).

The LOI is the prospect's letter to you that describes the key terms under which the prospect may buy the business if everything checks out during due diligence.

How long will the due diligence period last? Typically, 60 to 90 days so that a prospect has time to fully evaluate your company.

Now if you agree to the LOI's terms, it does not mean that a sale is going to happen. Some potential deals fall apart during due diligence.

In fact, a LOI is almost always *non-binding*, i.e. it gives the prospect many ways to walk away from the deal during the due diligence period.

Breakup Fees

Because potential deals can fall apart during due diligence, you may want to insist there's an agreement to pay you a breakup fee if the prospect doesn't go through with the purchase.

This fee compensates you for the time your business is held off the market while the prospective buyer performs due diligence before deciding to walk away from the deal.

However, this fee is discretionary. In fact, if you're a desperate seller, it's hard to insist upon a breakup fee when responding to the prospect's LOI.

On the other hand, if you're in no hurry to sell, or the prospect already owns a business that competes with your company, a breakup fee is a good way to partially protect yourself.

Chapter 5 - Prospective Buyer's Due Diligence

If you come to an agreement to sell based upon the prospective buyer's letter of intent (LOI), the prospect will have the period of time identified in the agreement to perform due diligence. During this due diligence period, here are some common topics about which the prospect may request information from you and your sales team about your company.

- Financial Records
- Assets and Liabilities
- Intellectual Property
- Ownership of Business Assets
- Ownership of Company Equity
- Silent Partners in Your Business
- Creditors and Debtors
- Lawsuits and Government Investigations

Your Internet lawyer and tax planner/accountant will work with you to provide the information the prospect truly needs while protecting information the prospect doesn't need to know. This is very important, particularly if the prospective buyer is a competitor who may merely be on a fishing expedition for insider information without any real desire to acquire your company.

Chapter 6 - Closing the Sale

Virtual Closing

If all goes well, the sale will occur. Unlike brick-and-mortar companies, selling your Internet business rarely involves everyone being in the same place to sign legal documents. Instead, you'll likely have a virtual closing.

This means each party will typically sign their documents separately at different locations. If you and the buyer are required to sign the same document, this is accomplished by having each party sign counterparts instead of a single copy signed by both. The signed documents will be shipped or emailed to the office where virtual closing will occur.

To make sure everything goes okay, you'll want to have the closing take place at your Internet business lawyer's office. This means all the documents will be reviewed by your legal counsel to make sure the "I's" are dotted and the "T's" are crossed so the sale goes according to the terms and conditions you agreed to.

If the buyer has an attorney, copies of the documents will go there too for review. Courtesy copies will be sent to any brokers involved in the deal.

Common Closing Documents

Here are common legal documents you may encounter at closing when you sell your Internet business.

- Purchase-and-Sale Agreement
- Escrow Agreement
- Spousal Consent to the Sale
- Bill of Sale
- Intellectual Property Assignment
- Equity Assignment
- Consulting Agreement
- Employment Agreement
- Noncompetition Agreement
- Non-disclosure/Confidentiality Agreement
- Resolutions Authorizing the Deal
- Certificates of Good Standing
- Tax Clearance Certificate
- Bulk Sale Documents
- Promissory Note
- Personal Guarantee
- Security Agreement
- Subordination Agreement
- UCC-1 Financing Statement

- Memorandum of Installment Sale

It's important to note you will not encounter all of these legal documents in your deal, just some of them.

Which ones you need will be determined by your Internet lawyer, the buyer's legal counsel, and any parties providing financing for the deal.

For example, if the sale is an asset deal, there probably won't be an equity assignment involved because your company is transferring assets instead of equity to the buyer.

Document Theft

Don't "borrow" legal documents you find online and repurpose them to sell your online business. Chances are the documents will not be structured to favor you. And they won't address all of the legal issues you need handled to protect yourself.

Plus, you risk legal liability for copyright infringement. For willful infringement, you could be liable to the documents' copyright owner for $150,000 statutory damages per violation, attorney fees, and court costs.

Broker Legal Forms

Broker closing legal forms are slightly better than "borrowing" someone else's legal documents. However, there are also significant legal risks to using broker legal forms too.

For example, if the documents are from the buyer's broker, they're designed to favor the purchaser instead of you as seller.

Even if the legal forms are from your broker, chances are they have gaps, missing key parts needed to protect you. And your broker's attorney will have prepared them to favor the broker in any dispute with you.

Your Internet business lawyer should prepare the documents designed to protect your interests. And if the documents are supplied by a broker or the buyer's legal counsel (not recommended), your attorney should review and revise them for your protection.

Chapter 7 - Post-Closing Activities

After the closing takes place, there will be many post-closing tasks that must be performed.

The exact tasks will vary depending upon how the deal is structured (e.g. asset purchase v. equity purchase). But each one should be done to ensure you're protected and the buyer is happy.

Seller's or buyer's remorse often occurs when someone drops the ball by not completing post-closing activities.

For example, if you fail to follow through with transfer of the company's domain name registrations, or the buyer makes late payments, you're risking expensive lawsuits where no one truly wins.

The best way to ensure things are done right is to create a checklist of post-closing tasks that must occur and follow through line by line until all items on the checklist are completed. Your checklist should contain due dates plus space for completion dates to be added as each task is done.

This checklist will make it easy for you and the buyer to get tasks done on a timely basis. In addition, it provides a quick reference guide when the buyer asks you as to the status of a particular item.

Although your sales team plays a key role in getting post-closing activities done, it's also your responsibility to make sure you've followed through with the deal as promised.

Quick Start Checklist

Here are three things to do in order to quickly get started selling your Internet company on favorable terms.

_____ 1. Put together your sales team, consisting of:

- a tax planner/accountant who knows ecommerce
- a reputable Internet business broker (note that there are brokers listed in the appendix to this guide)
- an experienced Internet business lawyer

_____ 2. Work with your sales team to determine a realistic asking price for your business as well as your bottom line.

_____ 3. Set criteria to prequalify prospective purchasers so that unqualified prospects don't waste your time.

Do You Need Help?

If you need legal help selling your online business, and you don't have an experienced Internet business lawyer you can rely upon, let's talk.

Go to https://mikeyounglaw.com/appointments/ or call 214-546-4247 to schedule your phone consultation.

Just choose a day and time that's convenient and I'll call you.

Wishing you the best.

-Mike

Michael E. Young, J.D., LL.M.
Attorney & Counselor at Law

About the Author

Since 1994, Internet Lawyer Mike Young has helped business clients prevent and solve legal problems.

President of the Internet Attorneys Association LLC, Mike has a law office in Plano, Texas (a Dallas suburb), and also serves as a foreign legal consultant in the Republic of Panama.

Happily married, Mike enjoys spending time with his family, walking his dogs, and self-defense training.

To learn more, go to MikeYoungLaw.com. While there, be sure to subscribe to his complimentary newsletter where you will receive important business legal news and tips by email.

Rate and Review

If you have found this guide helpful, please post a positive customer review for it at Amazon.com.

Whether you liked the guide or not, please send me a copy of the review you submitted to Amazon because feedback is important for updates and writing new guides too.

Just email a copy to me at mike@mikeyounglaw.com and I promise to respond.

Thank you.

-Mike

Glossary

ACCREDITED INVESTOR – For purposes of this guide, this is a high net worth individual or married couple that likely has the financial resources to acquire your Internet company. The criteria for being an accredited investor varies by country but typically is based upon either a high net worth or a multi-year history of high annual income.

ANGEL INVESTOR – A person who funds a prospective buyer of your business. This person is often either the buyer's friend or relative.

ASSET SALE – The sale of some or all of your Internet business' assets to a buyer. You retain your equity ownership (e.g. corporate stock) in the company that sold the assets. In contrast, see *Equity Sale*.

BREAKUP FEE – A fee that you and a prospect may agree that the prospect will pay to you under certain conditions if the prospect walks away without completing a purchase of your ecommerce business.

BUSINESS BROKER – A broker who represents either you or the buyer in the sale of your Internet company. Internet business brokers are often paid a commission for their services when the sale closes.

CLOSING – The time at which your Internet business is legally sold to the buyer. Closing involves various legal documents and at least partial payment of the sales price.

DISCRETIONARY EARNINGS – Rather than taking certain business revenues as earnings, you exercise your discretion to spend the funds on legitimate business expenses for your Internet company (e.g. a company vehicle lease). These discretionary earnings may be taken into account by a prospective buyer when valuing your business. See *Earnings Method*.

DUE DILIGENCE PERIOD – A time frame (often 60 to 90 days) where a prospective buyer of your ecommerce company will investigate your business before making a decision whether or not to go forward with the purchase.

EARNINGS METHOD – A way to value your Internet company based upon a multiple of your business' monthly or annual earnings. In contrast, see *Revenues Method*.

EQUITY SALE – The sale of some or all of the equity (e.g. corporate stock) in your Internet company to a buyer. The company retains the assets but the buyer now owns equity. In contrast, see *Asset Sale*.

INTERNET LAWYER – An experienced ecommerce business lawyer who will help reduce your risks and protect your legal rights as part of the sales process. Note that a buyer may also be represented by an Internet lawyer too.

LETTER OF INTENT (LOI) - a typically nonbinding letter from a prospective buyer that makes a tentative offer to purchase your Internet business if certain terms and conditions are met during a *Due Diligence Period*.

PROSPECTUS – A detailed overview of your Internet business that can be provided to certain qualified prospective buyers to review as part of evaluating your company.

REVENUES METHOD – A way to value your Internet company based upon a multiple of your business' monthly or annual revenues. In contrast, see *Earnings Method*.

RETURN ON INVESTMENT (ROI) – The ratio by which a prospective buyer (and the prospect's investors) guesstimates the profitability of investing in your business. There are multiple ways to calculate ROI.

SOPHISTICATED INVESTOR – See *Accredited Investor*.

VENTURE CAPITALIST – A professional investor who may be using third party funds to back a prospective buyer's purchase of your business. Unlike an *Angel Investor*, a venture capitalist rarely is related to or a friend of the prospective purchaser. The venture capitalist's focus is the *Return on Investment*.

Resources

Caution - just as technology changes quickly, so does the quality of service providers. What's a good resource today may become a poor or obsolete one tomorrow. In short, perform your own due diligence before using any of the following resources. Also note that each of these resources are listed in alphabetical order by topic, not by preference of the Author or Publisher of this guide.

Internet Business Brokers

App Business Brokers
Tel: 603-821-0928
Email: broker@appbusinessbrokers.com
Website: AppBusinessBrokers.com

FE International, Inc.
51 Melcher Street
1st Floor
Boston, MA 02210 USA
Tel: (855) 483-3547 (Toll Free)
Email: brokerage@feinternational.com
Website: FEinternational.com

Quiet Light Brokerage, Inc.
5802 Blackshire Path, Suite 103
Inver Grove Heights, MN 55076
Tel: 800-746-5034
Website: QuietLightBrokerage.com

Escrow Services

- Escrow.com

Digital Signature Services

- Adobe Sign - https://acrobat.adobe.com/us/en/sign/capabilities/digital-signatures.html
- Docusign - https://www.docusign.com/
- HelloSign - https://www.hellosign.com/

Disclosures and Disclaimers

This guide is published in print format. Neither the Author nor the Publisher makes any claim to the intellectual property rights of third party vendors, their subsidiaries, or related entities.

All trademarks and service marks are the properties of their respective owners. All references to these properties are made solely for editorial purposes. Except for marks actually owned by the Author or the Publisher, no commercial claims are made to their use, and neither the Author nor the Publisher is affiliated with such marks in any way.

Unless otherwise expressly noted, none of the individuals or business entities mentioned herein has endorsed the contents of this guide.

Limits of Liability & Disclaimers of Warranties

Because this guide is a general educational information product, it is not a substitute for professional advice on the topics discussed in it.

The materials in this guide are provided "as is" and without warranties of any kind either express or implied. The Author and the Publisher disclaim all warranties, express or implied, including, but not limited to, implied warranties of merchantability and fitness for a particular purpose. The Author and the Publisher do not warrant that defects will be corrected, or that any website or any server that makes this guide available is free of viruses or other harmful components. The Author does not warrant or make any representations regarding the use or the results of the use of the materials in this guide in terms of their correctness, accuracy, reliability, or otherwise. Applicable law may not allow the exclusion of implied warranties, so the above exclusion may not apply to you.

Under no circumstances, including, but not limited to, negligence, shall the Author or the Publisher be liable for any special or consequential damages that result from the use of, or the inability to use this guide, even if the Author, the Publisher, or an authorized representative has been advised of the possibility of such damages. Applicable law may not allow the limitation or exclusion of liability or incidental or consequential damages, so the above limitation or exclusion may not apply to you. In no event shall the Author's or Publisher's total liability to you for all damages, losses, and causes of action (whether in contract, tort, including but not limited to, negligence or otherwise) exceed the amount paid by you, if any, for this guide.

You agree to hold the Author and the Publisher of this guide, principals, agents, affiliates, and employees harmless from any and all liability for all claims for damages due to injuries, including attorney fees and costs, incurred by you or caused to third parties by you, arising out of the products, services, and activities discussed in this guide, excepting only claims for gross negligence or intentional tort.

You agree that any and all claims for gross negligence or intentional tort shall be settled solely by confidential binding arbitration per the American Arbitration Association's commercial arbitration rules. All arbitration must occur in the municipality where the Author's principal place of business is located. Your claim cannot be aggregated with third party claims. Arbitration fees and costs shall be split equally, and you are solely responsible for your own lawyer fees.

Facts and information are believed to be accurate at the time they were placed in this guide. All data provided in this guide is to be used for information purposes only. The information contained within is not intended to provide specific legal, financial, tax, physical or mental health advice, or any other advice whatsoever, for any individual or company and should not be relied upon in that regard. The services described are only offered in jurisdictions where they may be legally offered. Information provided is not all-inclusive, and is limited to information that is made available and such information should not be relied upon as all-inclusive or accurate.

For more information about this policy, please contact the Author at the e-mail address listed in the Copyright Notice at the front of this guide.

IF YOU DO NOT AGREE WITH THESE TERMS AND EXPRESS CONDITIONS, DO NOT READ THIS GUIDE. YOUR USE OF THIS GUIDE, PRODUCTS, SERVICES, AND ANY PARTICIPATION IN ACTIVITIES MENTIONED IN THIS GUIDE, MEAN THAT YOU ARE AGREEING TO BE LEGALLY BOUND BY THESE TERMS.

Affiliate Compensation & Material Connections Disclosure

This guide may contain hyperlinks to websites and information created and maintained by other individuals and organizations. The Author and the Publisher do not control or guarantee the accuracy, completeness, relevance, or timeliness of any information or privacy policies posted on these linked websites.

You should assume that all references to products and services in this guide are made because material connections exist between the Author or Publisher and the providers of the mentioned products and services ("Provider"). You should also assume that all hyperlinks within this guide are affiliate links for (a) the Author, (b) the Publisher, or (c) someone else who is an affiliate for the mentioned products and services (individually and collectively, the "Affiliate").

The Affiliate recommends products and services in this guide based in part on a good faith belief that the purchase of such products or services will help readers in general.

The Affiliate has this good faith belief because (a) the Affiliate has tried the product or service mentioned prior to recommending it or (b) the Affiliate has researched the reputation of the Provider and has made the decision to recommend the Provider's products or services based on the Provider's history of providing these or other products or services.

The representations made by the Affiliate about products and services reflect the Affiliate's honest opinion based upon the facts known to the Affiliate at the time this guide was published.

Because there is a material connection between the Affiliate and Providers of products or services mentioned in this guide, you should always assume that the Affiliate may be biased because of the Affiliate's relationship with a Provider and/or because the Affiliate has received or will receive something of value from a Provider.

Perform your own due diligence before purchasing a product or service mentioned in this guide.

The type of compensation received by the Affiliate may vary. In some instances, the Affiliate may receive complimentary products (such as a review copy), services, or money from a Provider prior to mentioning the Provider's products or services in this guide.

In addition, the Affiliate may receive a monetary commission or non-monetary compensation when you take action by clicking on a hyperlink in this guide. This includes, but is not limited to, when you purchase a product or service from a Provider after clicking on an affiliate link in this guide.

Purchase Price

Although the Publisher believes the price is fair for the value that you receive, you understand and agree that the purchase price for this guide has been arbitrarily set by the Publisher or the vendor who sold you this guide. This price bears no relationship to objective standards.

Due Diligence

You are advised to do your own due diligence when it comes to making any decisions. Use caution and seek the advice of qualified professionals before acting upon the contents of this guide or any other information. You shall not consider any examples, documents, or other content in this guide or otherwise provided by the Author or Publisher to be the equivalent of professional advice.

The Author and the Publisher assume no responsibility for any losses or damages resulting from your use of any link, information, or opportunity contained in this guide or within any other information disclosed by the Author or the Publisher in any form whatsoever.